For RJ, FHA, FJR, and FBL, and for our all young boys -
may they prayerfully discern whether God is calling them to
renew the Church by becoming holy priests.
K.W.

For my long-awaited Joseph,
that you will always have good, holy priests to look up to
M.W.

Text copyright © 2018 by Katie Warner
Illustrations copyright © 2018 Meg Whalen

All rights reserved. With the exception of short excerpts used in critical review, no part of this work may be reproduced, transmitted, or stored in any form whatsoever without the prior written permission of the publisher.

Book design by Meg Whalen
The text for this book is set in Kopius.
The illustrations for this book were rendered in colored pencil and gouache.

ISBN: 978-1-5051-1221-4

Published in the United States by
TAN Books
P.O. Box 410487
Charlotte, NC 28241
www.TANBooks.com

Printed in the United States of America

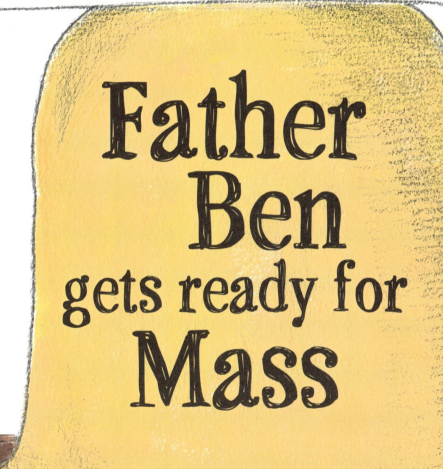

The sun is rising
and Father Ben hears the church bells ringing.
It's time to get ready for Mass!

Can you make the sound of a church bell?

Head to the church, Father Ben!

Trace your fingers along Father Ben's path to the front doors of his parish.

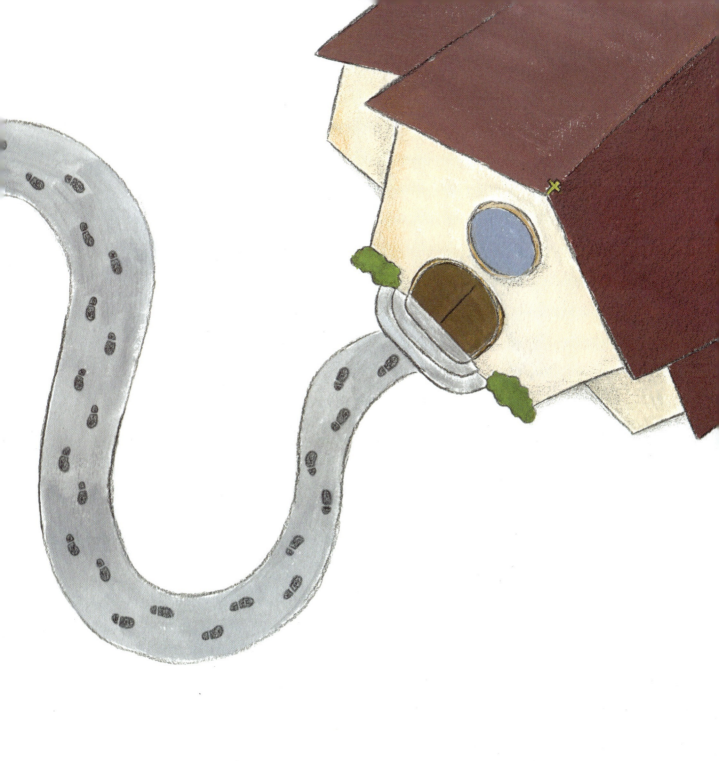

Inside the church,
Father Ben makes
the sign of the cross
with holy water
from the font.
Holy water reminds us
that we were baptized
in the name of the Father,
and of the Son,
and of the Holy Spirit.

Dip your finger in the
holy water font like
Father Ben. Now you make
the sign of the cross. Touch
your forehead, chest, and
each shoulder.

Before Father Ben gets ready for Mass,
he kneels and prays in the quiet church.
Father Ben remembers that, as a priest, he represents Jesus
for all of the people who will come to Mass.

Can you fold your hands in prayer before Mass?
Now say a simple prayer like this one:
"I love you, Jesus!"

It's time to head to the sacristy.
Here Father Ben looks at the Missal,
which helps him prepare for the Mass.

Point to the Missal for Father!
Do you need a little help finding it? Look for a red book.

Father Ben looks over the readings for today's Mass:
one from the Old Testament,
one from the Psalms,
one from the New Testament,
and one from the Gospel.

There will be readings from four different books of the Bible.
Can you hold up four fingers?

While he is still in the sacristy, Father Ben says special
prayers while he washes his hands
and puts on his vestments.
It's Ordinary Time, so that means he wears green.
Green is the color of hope and life.

Can you point to the green chasuble?

What other colors do you see?

The church is filled with people, and Mass is ready to begin!

Tilt the book to the left to help Father get to his position at the end of the procession!

Well done!
It looks like the altar servers need to light their candles...

Tap the candlewicks to light them!

Good. Time to celebrate the Mass, Father Ben!

The procession makes its way toward the altar.
How many people do you count in the procession?

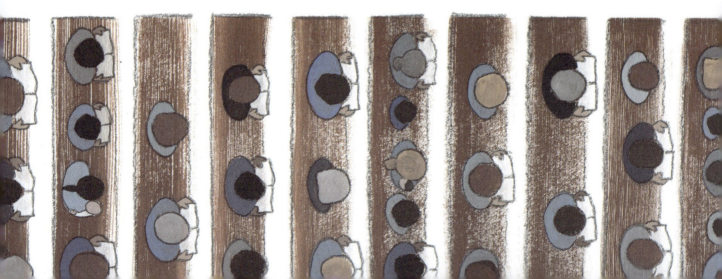

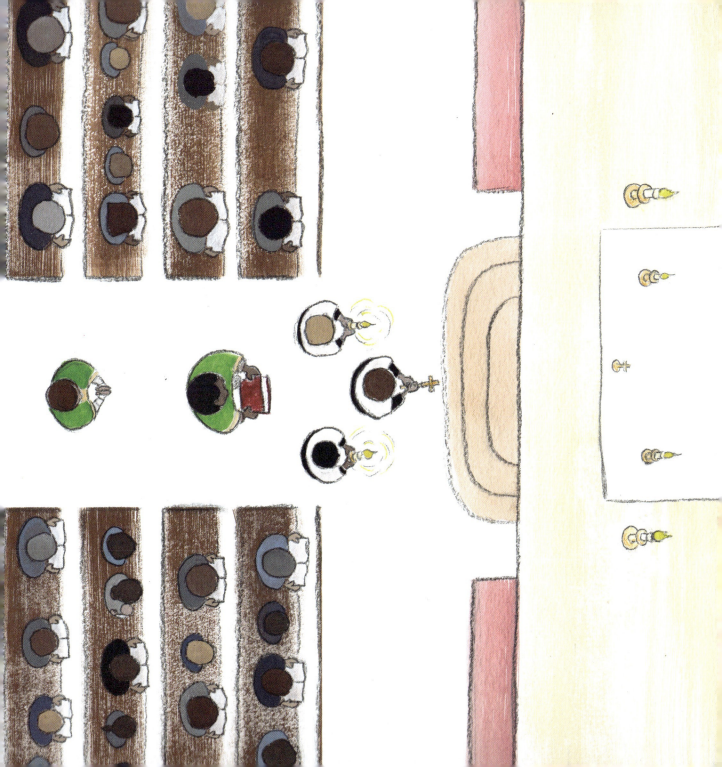

Father Ben kisses the altar,
where Jesus will soon be present in the Eucharist.

Now you kiss the altar, too!

During Mass, our eyes are watching, our ears are listening, our mouths are quiet, and our hearts are open.

Point to your watching eyes. Point to your listening ears. Point to your quiet mouth. Point to your open heart!

It's time for the Liturgy of the Word.
The lectors read from the Bible.
Before the Deacon proclaims the Gospel,
everyone stands and sings along.

Sing, "Alleluia, Alleluia, Alleluia!"

Father Ben and the people at Mass celebrate
the Liturgy of the Eucharist.
Father elevates the Sacred Host above his head.

Bow your head, and then raise it up again
to look at Jesus in the Holy Eucharist.

After the Liturgy of the Eucharist and as Mass comes to an end, Father Ben gives the people a blessing and recesses to the back of the church.

Help the altar servers blow out their candles.

Good.

Thank you for a beautiful Mass,
Father Ben!